HANUKKAH

95 316

HANUKKAH

by Miriam Chaikin

illustrated by Ellen Weiss

Holiday House/New York

Text copyright © 1990 by Miriam Chaikin
Illustrations copyright © 1990 by Ellen Weiss
ALL RIGHTS RESERVED
Printed in the United States of America
Library of Congress Cataloging-in-Publication Data
Chaikin, Miriam.
Hanukkah / written by Miriam Chaikin ;
illustrated in full color by Ellen Weiss. — 1st ed.
p.   cm.
Summary: Describes the history behind Hanukkah
and the ways it is celebrated.
ISBN 0-8234-0816-7
1. Hanukkah — Juvenile literature.   [1. Hanukkah.]
I. Weiss, Ellen, ill.   II. Title.
BM695.H3C44   1990
296.4'35—dc20   89-77512   CIP   AC
ISBN 0-8234-0816-7
ISBN 0-8234-0905-8 (pbk.)

For Jerusalem, rekindled in our time.
M.C.

To Mollie and Ken, with love.
E.W.

ong, long ago, cruel King Antiochus ruled the Jews of Israel. He wanted all people to worship the gods he worshiped. He said to the Jews: "Stop worshiping the one God that you love. You must worship the gods I worship—the god of the seas, the god of the sun, the god of fire, and all the others."

Mattathias Hasmon, a priest, was the leader of the Jews.

He answered:

"Our God is God over all gods. We will never do what you say."

Antiochus was angry. He set out to punish the Jews.

Their main place of worship was the Temple of God in Jerusalem. Antiochus sent his soldiers to ride through the Temple. They made it unfit for prayer.

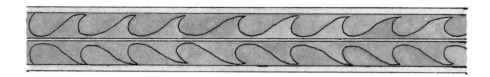

They dirtied the floor and put up a statue of Zeus, a Greek god. To honor Zeus, they gave him a gift of a roasted pig. The Temple was no longer holy. It was no longer pure.

Nor did Antiochus's cruelty end there. He passed a new law:

"Jews caught worshiping God, or teaching God's words, will be killed."

The king had already killed many Jews. He was certain to kill more.

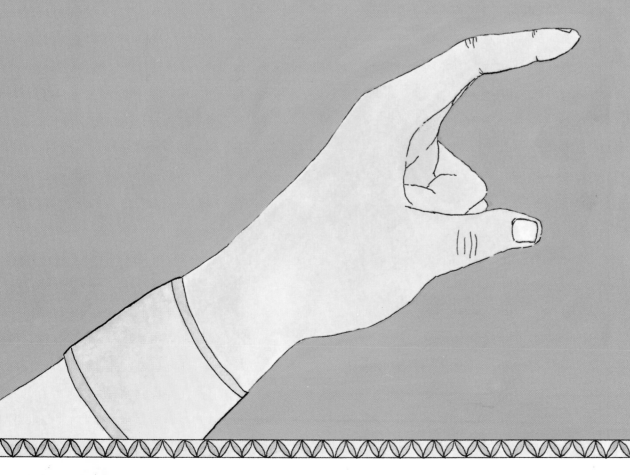

Enraged, the priest Mattathias and his sons went before the people and said, "We will not live as slaves under this madman. We will hide in the hills and fight from there."

The Jews left their homes and went to live in the hills, where they worshiped God and taught God's laws.

They also fought Antiochus's soldiers and fought well.
They were called *Maccabees,* a Hebrew word that means
good hitters.

Day in and day out, for three years, the Jews fought. They won more and more battles.

Try as he might, Antiochus could not defeat them. In the end, he and his soldiers went away.

Triumphant, the Jews hurried to Jerusalem. They made the Temple holy again. They swept and cleaned. They scrubbed and polished. And they found a surprise—a small jar of oil. It was not just any jar. The high priest's seal was still on it. That meant it was from before the war. The oil was still holy. Soon, the priests would be dedicating the Temple to God. They would have holy oil for the ceremony.

The dedication ceremony took place on the twenty-fifth day of the month of Kislev in the Jewish year 165 B.C.E. Jews came from far and wide to take part. They had much to celebrate. They had defeated Antiochus's mighty army. And Jerusalem was their capital city again.

The Jews had a second surprise. The holy oil in the little jar was a single portion, enough to burn for only one day. Yet it burned and burned and lasted eight days.

That celebration became a Jewish holiday for all time. It is called *Hanukkah*—a Hebrew word that means "dedicate." The holiday is celebrated for eight days, since that is how long the oil lasted. Jews all over the world celebrate Hanukkah in the same way.

Each night, they light a new candle in a *ha-nukkiah,* a nine-cup menorah or candle holder. The ninth cup is for the worker candle. It is lit first and then used to light the other holiday candles. And people thank and praise God.

They eat potato pancakes, or *latkes*, and other tasty Hanukkah foods.

They play "spin-the-dreidel"
and sing Hanukkah songs.

Everyone has a good time.